ARTIST ARCHIVES™ INTRODUCTION BY MAX ALLA

ELVGREN GIRLS 1

PORTLAND, OREGON

Design Principia Graphica
Technical Assistance Hoover H.Y. Li
Editor Ann Granning Bennett

The publisher would like to extend a special thanks to Ron Buol for
supplying various images in this book.

Printed in China

Library of Congress Cataloging-in-Publication Data
Collins, Max Allan.
　　Elvgren girls I / Max Allan Collins. — 1st American ed.
　　　　p. cm. — (Artist archives)
　　ISBN 1-888054-33-6 (pbk. : alk. paper)
　　1. Elvgren, Gillette. 2. Women in art 3. Pinup art — United
　　States. I. Title. II. Title: Elvgren girls 1. III. Title:
　　Elvgren girls one. IV. Series.
　　ND237.E585A4 1999
　　759.13 — dc21　　　　　　　　　　　　　　　99-28119
　　　　　　　　　　　　　　　　　　　　　　　　　CIP

9 8 7 6 5 4 3 2

FOR A FREE CATALOG WRITE TO COLLECTORS PRESS, INC.

P.O. Box 230986
Portland, Oregon 97281
Toll Free 800-423-1848
Or visit our website at *www.collectorspress.com*

ELVGREN
GIRLS I

INTRODUCTION

ALMOST TWO DECADES after his death, pin-up artist Gillette A. Elvgren has joined the exalted ranks of those long acknowledged masters of the form, Alberto Vargas and George Petty, and many critics and fans now consider the Midwestern-born artist to have been our premier purveyor of pulchritude. His all-American pin-up girls have joined the "Coca-Cola" Santa Clauses of his mentor Haddon Sundblom as images that are at once nostalgic icons and prime examples of twentieth-century illustration.

Gil Elvgren was born in St. Paul, Minnesota, on March 15, 1914. His Swedish immigrant father, Alex Aner Elvgren, a lumberjack, furniture maker, and carriage maker, had a soft-spoken, kind-hearted soul and an affinity for art. "Daddy Ake" came to own and operate a paint and wallpaper store with an art-supply area in the back, a store still in business in St. Paul, bearing a neon sign that echoes the famous signature shared by father and son. Elvgren's mother, Goldie Alice Gillette, a Wisconsin girl, was also artistically blessed. She and her twin sister performed as the Gillette Sisters, singing and dancing at Social Clubs and churches.

Only child Gil Elvgren displayed artistic talent early on and was considered a prodigy for his precocious sketches and woodcarving. Though for the most part an indifferent student, Gil was something of a whiz at math, and after graduating high school in 1932, he enrolled at the University of Minnesota to study architecture. Just a year later, however, at age 19 (and newly wed to his high school sweetheart, Janet Cummins), Elvgren moved to Chicago, where he studied at the American Academy of Art and found his way to the legendary Sundblom shop, working for the prestigious Stevens-Gross advertising agency.

Working in Sundblom's shop in Chicago with such future luminaries of illustration as Andrew Loomis and Al Buell, Elvgren contributed to numerous Coca-Cola ads himself, making fine use of the lush Sundblom brushstroke technique that makes Elvgren's girls — their skirts often blowing up for a generous glimpse of well-formed silk-clad limbs — such radiant wonders.

While pretty girls have been calendar subjects since around 1900, the pin-up is apparently one of the more pleasant by-products of World War Two. Wherever GIs went, they would "pin up" reminders of their girls back home.

Among the hometown snapshot-sweeties on the walls of barracks and bulkheads — whether in a prom gown or swimsuit, fetching reminders of what awaited Johnny when he eventually came marching home — were such Hollywood dream girls as a tightly-swimsuited Betty Grable or a lounging-in-lingerie Rita Hayworth or a sarong-slung Dorothy Lamour. The tradition of the calendar girl — that idealized vision of feminine beauty as imagined by illustrators for their advertising accounts — made a perfect fit with the longing of GIs for a glorified girl-next-door.

And glorifying the all-American girl-next-door was Gil Elvgren's specialty.

Following his first, uncharacteristic work (a Dionne Quints calendar) for Brown & Bigelow — where, a decade later, his long run of calendar girls would make his imagery if not his name familiar across America — Elvgren created his first series of pin-ups for Brown & Bigelow rival, the Louis F. Dow Company.

Elvgren's late 1930s work tended toward a deco style, and his subjects were often baby-faced, barely formed girls who echoed the Hollywood likes of Jean Harlow and Claudette Colbert. The wide-eyed blonde of "Forced Landing," for example, is only the most distant relative of the Brown & Bigelow beauties to come.

Not that these were not appealing, sexy pin-ups, thanks in part to the *art moderne* aspects of such works as "A Live Wire" (its telephone theme invoking Petty), "Short on Sails," "Sitting Pretty," and "Kneeding a Lift." But his deco-ish pin-ups changed in style as Elvgren and his girls moved into the 1940s, and he soon had developed the full-blown, Sundblom-influenced brush style that is virtually interchangeable with his more famous Brown & Bigelow work.

In these pin-ups — many of which are featured in this book — Elvgren transferred the apple-cheeked sweetie of Coca-Cola ads to the sort of calendar-girl pin-up favored by barbershops, car-repair shops, and lodge halls, adding the key element of Elvgren's subject matter, what the artist called the "compromising" situation.

An Elvgren girl exposes her supple, silk-stockinged limbs unintentionally, often to her embarrassment, though never humiliation. Behind her lovely face with its pucker of kiss-like embarrassment, an Elvgren girl is so confident in her charms that she doesn't mind showing them off a little, particularly if there's a gusty day or frisky pup on a leash to take the blame.

On occasion, Elvgren and his girls would dispense with the pretense of propriety, and a lovely, barely clad lass might gaze at us directly, unashamedly, even smilingly, as if caught by her husband or lover in the act of dressing or undressing, and not minding terribly. Even in these bolder pin-ups, Elvgren and his pretty subjects never come across as lascivious, the Coca-Cola-sweet smiles belonging to "nice girls," as the artist insisted all of his creations were.

While embarrassment (feigned or otherwise) remained a recurring Elvgren theme, as time went on, many of his "compromised cuties" seemed not to mind sharing their comeliness with a crowd. The show-business beauty of "Lucky Dog," for example, and the foxy fencer of "Foil Proof," make no apologies for their overexposed pulchritude. The boxing beauty of "Knockout" — one of the earliest examples of Elvgren hitting his stride — combines a wholesome subject with the almost jarring sexuality of her braless breasts and the suggestive design and shape of her shorts.

In "Tail Wind," a particularly lovely Dow pin-up, the beauty in a bright yellow bonnet and dress beams at us rather proudly, as the combined wind of a spring day and the propellers of an airplane reveal perfect limbs in nylons and garters. Beyond the subject matter, "Tail Wind" reveals an artist already at the top of his form, and the dominant yellow against the white clouds and blue of the sky is a strikingly limited yet vital color combination to which the artist would frequently return, The radiance of his girl in yellow makes her the sun at the center of the perfect, if breezy, day.

Even in the earlier "A Perfect Pair" — in which the artist is moving away from the formative baby-face deco cuties of the 1930s into the more mature, womanly subjects of the 1940s — his brunette subject merely smiles when her dress gets caught in the leash of the dog she's walking. Again, Elvgren uses a limited palette, and the solid green of the background typically pops his pin-up girl out at the viewer.

These compromising situations were an outgrowth of the pin-up girl's roots in the panel cartoon. The most famous pin-up artist of Elvgren's time was, of course, George Petty, whose world-famous "Petty Girls" grew out of a long series of cartoons in *Esquire* magazine in which various aging, pudgy (and obviously rich) would-be Romeos courted showgirls and starlets and golddiggers. These were unabashedly panel cartoons. When over time, the pudgy rich Romeos vanished, leaving the lounging Petty girls twisting their torsos and phone cords to the delight of the *Playboy* precursor's male audience, the pin-ups were still accompanied by a gag-cartoon caption.

Elvgren's "Miss-Placed Confidence," in which a beauty in her undies scolds a puppy for mistaking a coat tree for a real tree, is a typical example of the calendar girl's cartoon roots. An overtly comic element accompanies many an Elvgren painting — witness the sumptuously mature example of Elvgren's art, "What's Cooking," with its cute dog, stowaway penguin, and busty (and possibly braless) golden-blonde.

From the earliest days of the World War Two, Elvgren's girls were grist for the mills of amateur aviator artists decorating nose cones and flight jackets. The most frequently borrowed pin-up image on US military aircraft during the war was undoubtedly Vargas' "Sleepy Time Gal," a yawning blonde ready for bed; but the next most popular image was probably Elvgren's "Double Exposure."

And "Double Exposure," for obvious reasons, remains one of Elvgren's most enduringly popular early pin-ups. Despite its revealing (and atypical) nudity, "Double Exposure" has a certain sweetness, due to its genuinely surprised subject. Elvgren rarely indulged in such voyeuristic subjects, although another Peeping-Tom pin-up, "Peek-A-View," prefigures the keyhole pin-ups of Peter Driben and is a rare "faceless" Elvgren pose.

The Louis Dow Company got its money's worth out of Elvgren's first group of pin-ups. For many years after the artist had gone onto the more profitable pastures of Brown & Bigelow, Dow recycled the Elvgren pin-ups; staff artist Vaughn Bass would re-work and update the paintings, varying subject matter and apparel. Bass was himself a gifted pin-up artist and most of these so-called "overpaints" are pleasing to the eye, if rarely an improvement over the original.

Ironically, Elvgren created most of his so-called "wartime" pin-ups before the war, starting in 1937, published originally as calendar images and "mutoscope" cards (postcard-like vending-machine pin-ups), the paintings were re-published in a 8" by 10" format and collected into loose-leaf packets for shipment to military personnel both overseas and stateside.

These 8" by 10" images were perfect for pinning up by soldiers and sailors. The Dow Elvgren pin-ups were among the earliest and most widely distributed pin-ups of World War Two (it wasn't until the later years of the war that the *Esquire* Vargas images became widely seen and admired by servicemen).

Even in the early, sometimes formative works of this volume, Elvgren reveals himself as the quintessential American pin-up artist. His girl-next-door subject matter was much more appealing to the displaced hometown boys of World War Two than the more sophisticated fantasies of Petty and Vargas. Elvgren's sexy yet wholesome images spoke to something deeper in them. They touched emotions that simply were not part of Petty's Buick-sleek babes or Vargas' sometimes over-idealized Greek Goddesses.

From soft-drink ads to calendar pin-ups, Elvgren helped shape the image of the perfect girl-next-door in the minds and hearts of soldiers, sailors, and flyboys. By war's end, when American boys returned home to their girls and their families and their friends, one friend waiting for them was Gil Elvgren. And the artist used that very subject matter for memorable images of returning GIs romancing their Coke-sipping sweethearts, the Coca-Cola Company celebrating "the joyous homecoming of American soldiers" under such soft-sell slogans as "Just Like Old Times" and "Home — Refreshment."

Elvgren was an officer in that battalion of artists who created the idealized woman every man was fighting for, that perfect sensual, romantic dream of the postwar wife. As the postwar years faded into the 1950s, Elvgren continued to chronicle that perfect girl/woman, whether in his Brown & Bigelow calendar paintings or the more prosaic but no less idealized women of his advertising illustrations who smiled at yearning men from magazines, newspapers, and billboards.

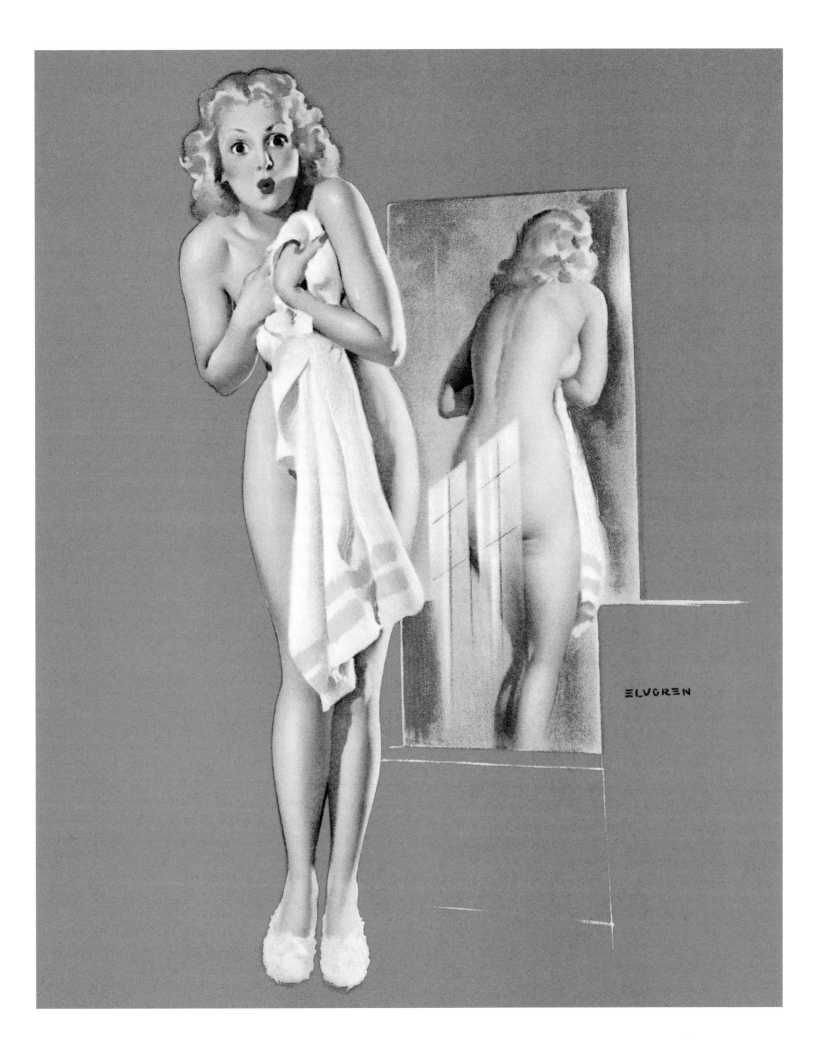